# USEFUL EXPRESSIONS

# in JAPANESE

## FOR THE ENGLISH–SPEAKING TOURIST

Edited by: Avraham J. Sivan and Yutaka Ikeda

·K·U·P·E·R·A·R·I

This booklet is an up-to-date and practical phrase book for your trip to Japan. It includes the phrases and vocabulary you will need in most of the situations in which you will find yourself, and it contains a pronunciation guide for all the material. Some of the phrases occur in more than one section so that you do not have to turn pages back and forth.

More polite forms are marked by asterik (*).

At the end are given some Japanese sayings, including those related to **Tabi** ("trip").

The pronunciation of Japanese is fairly simple. With one or two exceptions the sounds are similar to English sounds.

VOWELS:
- **a** like **a** in f**a**ther
- **e** like **e** in b**e**t
- **i** like **ee** in s**ee**
- **o** like **o** in c**o**mb
- **u** like **u** in p**u**ll

SEMI-VOWELS:
- **w** which for practical purposes occurs only before the vowel **a**
- **y** like **y** in **y**ard

CONSONANTS:
- **b** |b|
- **ch** like **ch** in **ch**oice
- **d** |d|
- **f** for which both lips come close together as if for blowing; the upper teeth should not touch the lips like English **f**. It is used only in **fu** except in the case of loan-words.
- **g** |g| when it begins a word, but when it is not the initial letter – a sound similar to the **ng** in si**ng**er in rapid pronunciation
- **h** |h|, but this always becomes **f** before the vowel **u**
- **j** like **j** in **j**oin
- **k** |k|
- **m** |m| and always followed by a vowel

**n** |n|

**p** |p|

**r** Japanese **r** is like neither **r** nor **l** in English but is sort of between the two; it is closer to **l** in words like lead, let, lot

**s** |s|

**sh** like **sh** in English

**t** |t|

**ts** like **ts** in cats and always followed by the vowel **u**

**z** like **ds** in words

# CONTENTS

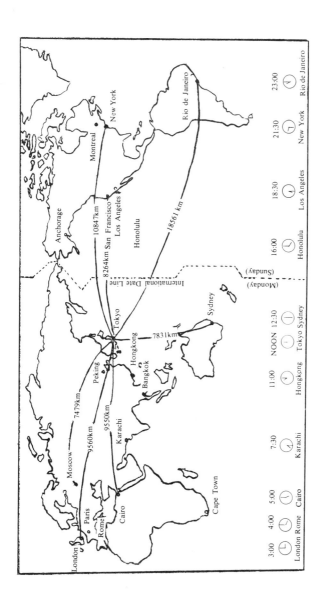

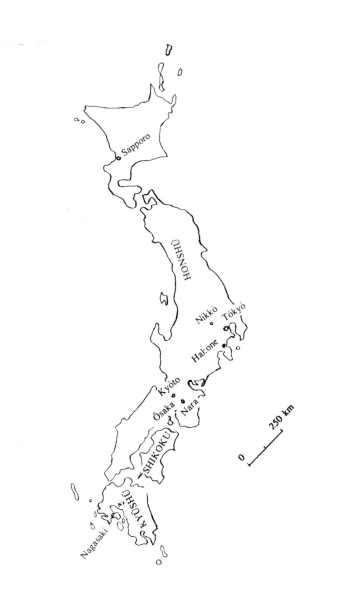

Sapporo

HONSHŪ

Nikkō Tōkyō

Hakone

Kyōto

Ōsaka Nara

SHIKOKU

250 km

0

KYŪSHŪ

Nagasaki

| Yes | Hai | はい |
| No | Iie | いいえ |
| Please | Dōzo | どうぞ |
| Please come in | Dōzo ohairi kudasai | どうぞ お入り下さい |
| Please sit down | Dōzo okake kudasai | どうぞ おかけ下さい |
| Thank you | Arigatō | ありがとう |
| " " | Arigatō gozaimasu* | ありがとうございます |
| Thank you very much | Dōmo arigatō | どうも ありがとう |
| " " | Dōmo arigatō gozaimasu* | どうも ありがとうございます |
| It was very kind of you | Dōmo arigatō gozaimashita | どうも ありがとうございました |
| | | |
| Not at all | Dō itashimashite | どういたしまして |
| Pardon! | Shitsurei! | 失礼！ |
| Excuse me! | Gomen-nasai! | 御免なさい！ |
| Excuse me, (but) … | Shitsurei desu ga … | 失礼ですが…… |
| You are welcome | Iie dō itashimashite | いいえ どういたしまして |
| I beg your pardon | Shitsurei, mō ichido o-negai -shimasu | 失礼 もう一度お願いします |

## GREETINGS

| | | |
|---|---|---|
| Good morning | Ohayō gozaimasu | おはようございます |
| Good day | Konnichi wa | こんにちは |
| Good evening | Konban wa | 今晩は |
| Good night | Oyasumi-nasai | おやすみなさい |
| Good-bye | Sayōnara | さようなら |
| See you later | Dewa mata nochi-hodo | では またのちほど…… |
| See you again | Mata o-ai-shimashō | またお会いしましょう |
| How are you? | O-genki desu ka? | お元気ですか？ |
| Fine, thank you | Hai genki desu | はい 元気です |
| And you | Anata wa (o-genki desu ka)? | あなたは（お元気ですか）？ |

あいさつ

## QUESTIONS

| | | |
|---|---|---|
| Where? | Doko desu ka? | どこ ですか？ |
| Where is ....? | ... wa doko desu ka? | …はどこ ですか？ |
| Where are ....? | "     " | "     " |
| When? | Itsu desu ka? | いつ ですか？ |

質　　問

2

|  |  |  |
|---|---|---|
| What? | Nan deshō ka? | 何でしょうか？ |
| How? | Dono-yō-ni shitara? | どのようにしたら？ |
| How much/many | Dono-kurai desu ka? | どのくらいですか？ |
| How much (price)? | Ikura desu ka? | いくらですか？ |
|  | O-ikura desu ka?* | おいくらですか？ |
| Who? | Dare (desu ka)? | だれ（ですか）？ |
|  | Donata desu ka?* | どなたですか？ |
| Which? | Dochira desu ka? | どちらですか？ |
| Which...? | Dono ... desu ka? | どの......ですか？ |
|  | Dochira-no ... desu ka?* | どちらの......ですか？ |
| Why? | Naze (desu ka)?/Dōshite desu ka? | なぜ（ですか）？/どうして（ですか）？ |
| Because ... | (Nazenara) ... kara desu | （なぜなら）......からです |

## WHAT DO YOU CALL ... IN JAPANESE?

英語で何と いいますか

|  |  |  |
|---|---|---|
| Excuse me, what do you call this?/that in Japanese? | Sumimasen ga kore wa nihon-go de nan to iimasu ka? | すみませんが、これは日本語で何といいますか？ |
| This/These | Kore wa | これは |

|  |  |  |
| --- | --- | --- |
| It | Sore wa | それは |
| That/Those | Are wa | あれは |
| Excuse me, how do you say | Sumimasen ga 'beautiful'-o | すみませんが……を日本 |
| 'beautiful' in Japanese? | nihon-go de nanto iimasu ka? | 語で何といいますか？ |
| Beautiful | Utsukushii | 美しい |
| We say – 'utsukushii' | 'Utsukushii' desu | "美しい"です |
| A little/A lot | Sukoshi/Takusan | 少し/沢山 |
| And | Soshite | そして |
| ... and xxx | ... to xxx | ……と××× |
| Beautiful/Ugly | Utsukushii/Minikui | 美しい/醜い |
| Better/Worse | Yori yoi (Motto ii)/Yori warui (Motto warui) | より良い（もっといい）/より悪い（もっと悪い） |
| Big/Small | Ōkii/Chiisai | 大きい/小さい |
| Bigger/Smaller | Motto ōkii/Motto chiisai | もっと大きい/もっと小さい |
| Cheap/Expensive | Yasui/Takai | 安い/高い |
| Cheaper/More expensive | Motto yasui/Motto takai | もっと安い/もっと高い |
| Early/Late | Hayai/Osoi | 早い/遅い |
| Earlier/Later | Motto hayaku/Motto osoku | もっと早く/もっと遅く |
| Easy/Difficult | Yasashii/Muzukashii | やさしい/むずかしい |
| Easier/More difficult | Motto yasashii/Motto muzukashii | もっとやさしい/もっとむずかしい |
| Enough/Deficient | Jūbun/Fujūbunna | 十分/不十分な |

4

|  |  |  |
|---|---|---|
| Fast/Slowly | Hayaku/Yukkuri | 早く／ゆっくり |
| Free (vacant)/Occupied | Aite-iru/Shiyō-chū | 空いている／使用中 |
| Full/Empty | Ippai/Kara | 一杯／空（から） |
| Full (no room) | Man'in | 満員 |
| Good/Bad | Yoi(Ii)/Warui | 良い（いい）／悪い |
| Heavy/Light | Omoi/Karui | 重い／軽い |
| Heavier/Lighter | Motto omoi/Motto karui | もっと重い／もっと軽い |
| Here/There | Koko/Asoko | ここ／あそこ |
| Here it is/There it is | Koko desu/Asoko desu | ここです／そこです |
| Hot/Cold | Atsui/Tsumetai | 熱い／冷たい |
| Hotter/Colder | Motto atsui/Motto tsumetai | もっと熱い／もっと冷たい |
| Maybe | Tabun | 多分 |
| Many (Much) | Takusan | 沢山 |
| Many ...(Much ...) | Takusan-no ... | 沢山の |
| More/Less | Motto ōku/ Motto sukunaku | もっと多く／もっと少なく |
| Near/Far | Chikai/Tōi | 近い／遠い |
| Nearer/Farther | Yori chikai (Motto chikai)/Yori tōi (motto tōi) | より近い（もっと近い）／より遠い（もっと遠い） |
| The nearest | Ichiban chikai | 一番近い…… |
| Next/Last | Tsugi no/Saigo no | 次の／最後の |
| Now/Then | Ima/Sono toki | 今／その時 |
| Of course | Mochiron | もちろん |

|  |  |  |
|---|---|---|
| Often/Seldom | Shibashiba/Metta-ni ... nai | しばしば/めったに… ない |
| Old/New | Furui/Atarashii | 古い/新しい |
| Older/Newer | Yori furui (Motto furui)/Yori atarashii (Motto atarashii) | より古い（もっと古い）/より新しい（もっと新しい） |
| Old/Young | Toshitotta/Wakai | 年とった/若い |
| Older/Younger | Yori toshitotta (Motto toshitotta)/Yori wakai (Motto wakai) | より年とった（もっと年とった）/より若い（もっと若い） |
| Open/Closed | Aite-iru/Shimatte-iru | 開いている/閉まっている |
| Perhaps | Aruiwa (Hyotto suru to) | あるいは、ひょっとすると |
| Probably | Tabun | 多分 |
| Or (... or xxx) | Matawa (... matawa xxx) | または（…または×××） |
| Quick/Slow | Hayai/Yukkuri-shita | 早い/ゆっくりした |
| Right/Left | Migi/Hidari | 右/左 |
| Right/Wrong | Tadashii/Machigatta | 正しい/まちがった |
| Some | Ikutsuka | いくつか |
| Somebody (Someone) | Aru hito, Dare ka | ある人、誰か |
| Someday | Aru hi | ある日 |
| Somehow | Nanto-naku | なんとなく |
| Something | Nanika, Aru mono | 何か、あるもの |
| Sometime˙ | Itsuka | いつか |
| Sometimes | Tokidoki | 時々 |

| | | |
|---|---|---|
| Soon | Mamonaku | まもなく |
| Too (Also) | ... mo mata | ……も また |
| Very | Taihen | 大変 |
| Very expensive | Taihen takai | 大変高い |

## DO YOU SPEAK ...?

| | | |
|---|---|---|
| | | …を話しますか |
| Do you speak English? | Ei-go-o hanashimusu ka? | 英語を話しますか？ |
| English | Ei-go | 英語 |
| French | Furansu-go | フランス語 |
| German | Doitsu-go | ドイツ語 |
| Italian | Itarī-go | イタリー語 |
| Spanish | Supein-go | スペーン語 |
| Arabic | Arabia-go | アラビア語 |
| Chinese | Chugoku-go | 中国語 |
| Japanese | Nihon-go | 日本語 |
| Do you understand ...? | ... ga o-wakari desu ka? | ……がおわかりですか？ |
| Do you understand English? | Ei-go ga o-wakari desu ka? | 英語がおわかりですか？ |
| Yes, I understand | Hai wakarimasu | にい、わかります |

Yes, I understand a little     Hai sukoshi wakarimasu     はい　少しわかります

I am sorry …     Zannen desu ga …     残念ですが……

I am sorry, I don't understand     Zannen desu ga wakarimasen     残念ですがわかりません

I don't speak Japanese well     Watashi wa nihongo ga amari yoku dekimasen     私は日本語があまりよくできません

Could you please speak more slowly?     Mō-sukoshi yukkuri shabette itadake-masu ka?     もう少しゆっくりしゃべっていただけますか？

---

**COULD YOU KINDLY WRITE... DOWN ON THE PAPER?**

（すみませんが）……を紙に書いていただけませんか

---

Could you kindly write it down?     (Sumimasen ga) sore o kami ni kaite itadakemasu ka?     （すみませんが）それを紙に書いていただけますか？

A word     Tango     単語

The word     Sono tango     その単語

Expression     Iimawashi (Hyōgen)     いいまわし、表現

The expression     Sono iimawashi (hyōgen)     そのいいまわし、表現

The phrase     Sono kotoba-zukai     その言葉づかい

Yes, I'll write it down     Hai o-kaki-shimashō     はい　お書きをしましょう

8

Could you kindly translate this for me/us?
すみませんが　これを訳していただけますか？

Please point to this phrase in this book
その言葉づかいが　この本の中にあったら教えて下さい

Just a minute, I'll see if I can find it in the book
ちょっとお待ち下さい　調べてみましょう

Is there anyone here who speaks Enlish?
どなたか英語のできる方が、いらっしゃいますか？

Yes, there is
はい、おります

Yes?! That's fine
いらっしゃいますか？！それはすばらしい

Is it a lady or a man?
それは女の方ですか、男の方ですか？

It is a man
男の方です

Could you kindly call him here?
すみませんが　その方をここに呼んでいただけますか？

---

Sumimasen ga kore-o yakushite itadake masu ka?

Sono kotoba-zukai ga kono hon nonakani attara oshiete kudasai

Chotto o-machi kudasai shirabetemimashō

Donata ka ei-go no dekirukata ga irasshai masu ka?

Hai ori masu

Irasshai masu ka?! Sore wa subarashii

Sore wa onna no-kata desu ka, otoko no-kata desu ka?

Otoko no kata desu

Sumimasen ga sono-kata o koko ni yonde itadakemasu ka?

# WHERE IS THE NEAREST ...?

ここから一番近い ……はどこですか

すみませんが ここから一番 近い……はどこですか?

この近くに……がありますか

|  |  |  |
|---|---|---|
| Excuse me, where is the nearest ...? | Sumimasen ga koko kara ichiban chikai ... wa doko desu ka? | |
| Do you know any...nearby? | Kono chikaku ni ... ga arimasu ka? | |
| Antique shop | Kottō-ya | こっとう屋 |
| Art gallery | Bijutsu-kan | 美術館 |
| Bank | Ginkō | 銀行 |
| Barber shop | Rihatsu-ten, Sanpatsu-ya | 理髪店、散髪屋 |
| Beauty parlor | Biyo-in | 美容院 |
| Book shop | Hon-ya | 本屋 |
| Camera shop | Kamera-ten | カメラ店 |
| Dentist | Shika-i-in | 歯科医院 |
| Department store | Depāto | デパート |
| Draper | Fukuji-ten | 服地店 |
| Dressmaker's | Yōsai-ten | 洋裁店 |
| Drug store | Yakkyoku | 薬局 |
| Fruit shop | Kudamono-ya | 果物屋 |
| Fish shop | Sakana-ya | 魚屋 |

10

|  |  |  |
|---|---|---|
| Garrage | Garēji | ガレージ（自動修理所） |
| Green grocer's | Aomono-ya | 青物屋 |
| Grocer's (store) | Kanbutsu-ya | 乾物屋 |
| Hat shop | Bōshi-ten | 帽子店 |
| Hospital | Byōin | 病院 |
| Laundry | Kurīningu-ya | クリーニング屋 |
| Liquor store | Saka-ya | 酒屋 |
| Pharmacy | Yakkyoku | 薬局 |
| Photographer's | Shashin-ya | 写真屋 |
| Police station | Keisatsu | 警察 |
| Post office | Yūbin-kyoku | 郵便局 |
| Shoe shop | Kutsu-ya | 靴屋 |
| Station | Eki | 駅 |
| Stationery's shop | Bunbōguten | 文房具店 |
| Super market | Sūpā-māketto | スーパーマーケット |
| Toilet | Toire, Tearai | トイレ、手洗い |
| Toy shop | Omocha-ya | おもちゃ屋 |
| Travel agent | Ryokōsha | 旅行社 |
| Watch maker | Tokei-ya | 時計屋 |

| BANK | | 銀　行 |
|---|---|---|
| Excuse me, where is the nearest bank? | Kono chikaku ni ginkō ga arimasu ka? | この近くに銀行がありますか？ |
| Yes, there is one right there | Hai sugu soko ni ari masu | はい、すぐそこにあります |
| Right there | Sugu sokoni | すぐそこに |
| On that corner | Ano kado ni | あの角に |
| On the next street | Tsugi no tōrini | 次の通りに |
| I want change some dollars | Doru-o sukoshi kaetai-no desu ga | ドルを少し替えたいのですが |
| Dollars | Doru | ドル |
| Marks | Maruku | マルク |
| Pounds | Pondo | ポンド |
| Francs | Furan | フラン |
| Travellars's cheques | Toraberu-chekku | トラベルチェック（旅行小切手） |
| Passport | Pasupōto | パスポート |
| Can I see your passport, please? | Pasupōto o misete itadakemasu ka? | パスポートをみせていただけますか？ |
| Here it is | Hai koko ni arimasu | はい、ここにあります |
| Could I have it in small change, please? | Chiisai o-satsu de itadakemasu ka? | 小さいお札でいただけますか？ |
| In large notes | Ōkii o-satsu de | 大きいお札で |

12

## HOTEL

| English | Romaji | Japanese |
|---|---|---|
| I am looking for a good hotel | Ii hoteruo sagashiteimasu | いいホテルを さがしており ます |
| Not so expensive | Amari takakunai | あまり高くない |
| Do you know any good hotel nearby? | Dokoka kono chikakuni ii hoteru o gozonji desu ka? | どこかこの近くにといいホテル をご存知ですか？ |
| My name is x x x | xxx-to ii-masu ga ... | ×××といいますが…… |
| I booked a room here | Heya o yoyaku shite-aru hazu desu ga ... | 部屋を予約してあるはずです が |
| Single | Shinguru | シングル |
| Double | Daburu | ダブル |
| I should like to see the room | Heya o mitai no desu ga ... | 部屋を見たいのですが…… |
| On which floor is my room? | Watashi no heya wa nankai desu ka? | 私の部屋は可階ですか？ |
| It is on the first floor | Ikkai desu | 一階です |
| It is on the second floor | Nikai desu | 二階〃 |
| It is on the third floor | Sangai desu | 三階〃 |
| It is on the fourth floor | Yonkai desu | 四階〃 |
| It is on the fifth floor | Gokai desu | 五階〃 |
| Is the room air-conditioned? | Sono heyaniwa kūrā ga tsuiteimasu ka? | その部屋にはクーラーがつい ていますか？ |

13

| English | Romaji | Japanese |
|---------|--------|----------|
| Yes, it is air-conditioned | Hai, tsuite imasu | はい、ついています |
| Has the room a private bath or shower? | Heya ni wa furo ka shawā ga tsuiteimasu ka? | 部屋には風呂か、シャワーがついていますか？ |
| Yes, it has | Hai, tsuiteimasu | はい、ついています |
| Is it with breakfast? | Chōshoku-tsuki desu ka? | 朝食付ですか？ |
| How much per day? | Ichinichi ikura desu ka? | 一日いくらですか？ |
| Do you have a bigger room？ | Motto ōkina heya wa arimasu ka? | もっと大きな部屋はありますか？ |
| Smaller | Motto chīsana | もっと小さな |
| Cheeper | Motto yasui | もっと安い |
| Quieter | Motto shizukana | もっと静かな |
| Will you send for my bag? | Kaban o heya ni hakonde itadakemasu ka? | カバンを部屋に運んでいただけますか？ |
| My room key, please | Heya no kagi o kudasai | 部屋のかぎをください |
| Room key | Heya no kagi (room key) | 部屋のかぎ（ルームキー） |
| Room number | Heya no bangō | 部屋の番号（ルームナンバー） |
| Lift | Erebētā (Elevator) | エレベーター |
| Bed | Betto | ベット |
| Blanket | Mōfu | 毛布 |
| Sheet | Shitsu | シーツ |
| May I have another towel? | Taoru o mō ichimai moraemasu ka? | タオルをもう一枚もらえますか |

14

|  |  |  |
|---|---|---|
| May I have another blanket? | Mōfu o motto moraemasu ka? | 毛布をもっともらえますか？ |
| May I have more hangers? | Hangā o motto moraemasu ka? | ハンガーをもっともらえますか？ |
| May I have needles and cottons? | Hari to ito o moraemasu ka? | 針と糸をもらえますか？ |
| Toilet paper | Toiretto-pēpā | トイレットペーパー |
| Who is it? | Donata desu ka? | どなたですか？ |
| Please (come in)! | Dōzo (o-hairi kudasai) | どうぞ（お入り下さい） |
| Cable | Denpō | 電報 |
| Could you cable abroad for me? | Kokugai ni denpō o utte itadakemasu ka? | 国外に電報を打っていただけますか？ |
| I would like to call abroad | Kokusai-denwa o kaketai no desu ga … | 国際電話をかけたいのですが |
| International telephone | Kokusai-denwa | 国際電話 |
| Will you please wake me at six o'clock? | Rokuji ni okoshite itadakemasu ka? | 六時に起こしていただけますか？ |
| At half past six | Rokuji-han ni | 六時半に |
| At seven | Shichiji ni | 七時に |
| Where is the Dining Room? | Shokudō wa doko desu ka? | 食堂はどこですか？ |
| It is on the second floor | Nikai desu | 二階です |
| When can I get breakfast? | Chōshoku wa nanji kara desu ka? | 朝食は何時からですか？ |
| From seven o'clock | Shichiji kara desu | 七時からです |

15

|  |  |  |
|---|---|---|
| Is there a tennis court nearby? | Chikaku ni tenisu-kōto ga arimasu ka? | 近くにテニスコートがありますか？ |
| Where is the swimming pool? | Pūru wa doko desu ka? | プールはどこですか？ |
| Have you got any mail for me? | Watashi-ate ni tegami ga kite imasu ka? | 私宛に手紙が来ていますか？ |
| Is there any message for me? | Nani ka watashi-ate ni messēji ga kite-imasu ka? | なにか私宛にメッセージが来ていますか？ |
| I am going out and return at nine o'clock | Ima kara dekakete, ku-ji ni kaettekimasu | 今から出かけて 九時に帰ってきます |
| (I'll return) around ten o'clock | Jū-ji goro (kaette-kimasu) | 十時頃 |
| Around half past ten | Jū-ji-han goro | 十時半頃 |
| I'll leave the hotel tomorrow at five o'clock | Asu go-ji ni hoteru o demasu | 明日 五時にホテルを出ます |
| Tomorrow morning at six o'clock | Myōchō roku-ji ni | 明朝六時に |
| Please make up my bill | Kanjō o onegai shimasu | 勘定をお願いします |
| May I store my luggage here untill eleven o'clock? | Kaban o jū-ichi-ji made azukkatte itadakemasu ka? | カバンを十一時まであずかっていただけますか？ |
| Till noon | Jū-ni-ji made | 十二時まで |

16

# TRANSPORT

輸　送

| | | |
|---|---|---|
| Bus | Basu | バス |
| Train | Kisha | 汽車 |
| Electric train | Densha | 電車 |
| Express train | Kyūkō | 急行 |
| Plane | Hikōki | 飛行機 |
| Underground | Chikatetsu | 地下鉄 |
| Ticket | Kippu | 切符 |
| Driver | Untenshu, Doraibā | 運転手, ドライバー |
| Porter | Pōtā | ポーター |
| Load | Nimotsu | 荷物 |
| Luggage | Tenimotsu | 手荷物 |
| Taxi | Takushī | タクシー |
| Charge | Ryōkin | 料金 |

# RAILWAY STATION

箙

| English | Romaji | Japanese |
|---|---|---|
| Excuse me, where is the railway station? | Sumimasen ga kisha no eki wa doko desu ka? | すみませんが　汽車の駅はどこですか？ |
| Where is the ticket window? | Kippu-uriba wa doko desu ka? | 切符売場はどこですか？ |
| There it is | Soko desu | そこです |
| Here it is | Koko desu | ここです |
| Thank you very much | Dōmo arigatō gozaimashita | どうもありがとうございます |
| I'd like to have a bullet-train ticket for Kyōto | Kyōto iki Shinkansen no kippu o ichi-mai kudasai | 京都行き新幹線の切符を一枚下さい |
| One (ticket) | (Kippu o) ichi-mai | （切符を）一枚 |
| Two (tickets) | Ni-mai | 二枚 |
| Three (tickets) | San-mai | 三枚 |
| Four (tickets) | Yon-mai | 四枚 |
| Adult/Adults | Otona | 大人 |
| Child/Children | Kodomo | 子供 |
| Two (tickets) for adults, one for child | Otona ni-mai, kodomo ich-mai | 大人二枚、子供一枚 |
| One for adult and three for children | Otona ichi-mai to kodomo san-mai | 大人一枚と子供三枚 |
| One-way ticket | Katamichi kippu | 片道切符 |

18

| | | |
|---|---|---|
| Return ticket | Ōfuku kippu | 往復切符 |
| Seat | Seki | 席 |
| First class (seat) | "Gurĭn"-sha (lit. "green"-car) | グリーン車 |
| Ordinary (seat) | Futsū | 普通 |
| Sleeping-car | Shindai | 寝台車 |
| Berth ticket | Shindai-ken | 寝台券 |
| No smoking seat | Kin'en-seki | 禁煙席 |

## WHERE IS THIS PLACE?

ここはどこですか

| | | |
|---|---|---|
| Excuse me, where is this place? | Sumimasen ga koko wa doko desu ka? | すみませんが ここはどこで すか？ |
| This is Ōsaka | Ōsaka desu | 大坂です |
| Is this (place) Kyōto? | Koko wa Kyōto desu ka? | ここは京都ですか？ |
| Yes, it is | Hai, sō desu | はい、そうです |
| No, it isn't | Iie (chigai masu) | いいえ （ちがいます） |
| It is Nara | Nara desu | 奈良です |
| Is this Nikkō? | Koko wa Nikkō desu ka? | ここは日光ですか？ |
| No, Nikkō is the next station | Iie, Nikkō wa tsugi no eki desu | いいえ、日光は次の駅です |
| Oh, is it? | Ā, sō desu ka | ああ そうですか |

| English | Romaji | Japanese |
|---|---|---|
| Thank you very much | Dōmo arigatō gozaimashita | どうも ありがとうございました |
| You're welcome | Dō itashimashite | どういたしまして |

## PHARMACY 薬局

|  |  |  |
|---|---|---|
| Have you a mild cure for a cold? | Hana-kaze ni kiku kusuri ga ari masu ka? | 鼻風邪にきく薬がありますか? |
| Have you something for a headache? | Zutsū ni kiku kusuri ga arimasu ka? | 頭痛にきく薬がありますか? |
| Have you something for toothache? | Shitsū (or Haita) ni kiku kusuri ga arimasu ka? | 歯痛にきく薬がありますか? |
| Alcohol | Arukōru | アルコール |
| Aspirin | Asupirin | アスピリン |
| Bandage | Hōtai | 繃帯((ほうたい)) |
| Cotton wool | Dasshimen | 脱脂綿 |
| Iodione | Yōdo | ヨードチンキ |
| Mercurochrome | Aka-chin | 赤チン |
| Thermometer | Taion-kei | 体温計 |
| Vaselin | Waserin | ワセリン |

| DOCTORS | | |
|---|---|---|

医 者

| Get a doctor — quick! | Isha o yonde kudasai — Hayaku! | 医者を呼んで下さい一早く！ |
| Doctor/Doctors | Isha, Ishi | 医者, 医師 |
| Dentist | Shika-i | 歯科医 |
| Dermatologist (Skin specialist) | Hifuka-i | 皮膚科 |
| Ear, nose and throat specialist | Jibi-inkōka-i | 耳鼻・咽喉科医 |
| Eye specialist | Ganka-i | 眼科医 |
| Obsterician and Gynecologist | Sanfujinka-i | 産婦人科医 |
| Internal specialist | Naika-i | 内科医 |
| Neurologist | Shinkeika-i | 神経科医 |
| Orthopedist | Seikei-geka-i | 整形外科医 |
| Pediatrician | Shōnika-i | 小児科医 |
| Surgeon | Geka-i | 外科医 |
| Is there a doctor in the hotel? | Kono hoteru ni isha wa imasu ka? | このホテルに医者がいますか？ |
| Can you get me/us a doctor? | Isha o yonde-itadakemasu ka? | 医者を呼んでいただけますか？ |
| Quickly | Hayaku | 早く |
| Please telephone for a doctor immediately | Isha ni sugu denwa-shite-kudasai | 医者にすぐ電話して下さい |

| English | Romaji | Japanese |
|---|---|---|
| Do you know any doctor who speaks English? | Eigo no wakaru isha o gozonji desu ka? | 英語のわかる医者をご存知ですか？ |
| Do you know any American hospital? | Amerika-kei no byōin o gozonji desu ka? | アメリカ系の病院をご存知ですか？ |
| Could the doctor come and see me here? | Isha wa koko ni kite-mite-kureru no deshō ka? | 医者はここに来て診てくれるのでしょうか？ |
| What time can the doctor come? | Isha wa nanji ni koraremasu ka? | 医者は何時に来られますか？ |
| What's the trouble? | Doko ga warui no desu ka? | どこの具合が悪いのですか？ |
| Where's the pain? | Doko ga itamu no desu ka? | どこが痛むのですか？ |
| I am not feeling well | Kibun ga suguremasen | 気分がすぐれません |
| My husband is not well | Shujin no chōshi ga suguremasen | 主人の調子がすぐれません |
| My wife is not well | Kanai no chōshi ga suguremasen | 家内の調子がすぐれません |
| My/Our child is not well | Kodomo no chōshi ga suguremasen | 子供の調子がすぐれません |
| I've got backache | Senaka ga itamimasu | 背中が痛みます |
| I've got cold | Kaze o hikimashita | 風邪を引きました |
| I have a headache | Zutsū ga shimasu | 頭痛がします |
| I have a bad headache | Hidoi zutsū ga shimasu | ひどい頭痛がします |
| I've got stomachache | I ga itamimasu | 胃が痛みます |

22

|  |  |  |
|---|---|---|
| I've got temparature/fever | Netsu ga arimasu | 熱があります |
| I have no appetite | Shokuyoku ga arimasen | 食欲がありません |
| I feel shivery | Zokuzoku shimasu | ぞくぞくします |
| I feel dizzy | Memai ga shimasu | 目まいがします |
| I feel nausea | Hakike ga shimasu | 吐き気がします |
| I feel faint | Sottō shisō desu | 卒倒しそうです |
| Appendicitis | Chūyōsui-en (Mōchō-en) | 虫様垂炎（盲腸炎） |
| Asthma | Zensoku | ぜん息 |
| Bruise | Daboku-shō | 打撲傷 |
| Cold | Kaze | 風邪 |
| Constipation | Benpi | 便秘 |
| Convulsion | Keiren | けいれん |
| Cramps | Komuragaeri | こむらがえり |
| Diabetes | Tōnyōbyō | 糖尿病 |
| Diarrhoea | Geri | 下痢 |
| Dysentery | Sekiri | 赤痢 |
| Food poisoning | Shoku-chūdoku | 食中毒 |
| Hay fever | Kafun-shō | 花粉症 |
| Hernia | Herunia | ヘルニア |
| Indigestion | Shōka-furyō | 消化不良 |
| Inflammation of ... | ... no enshō | …の炎症 |
| Influenza | Infuruenza | インフルエンザ |

| English | Romaji | Japanese |
|---|---|---|
| Rheumatism | Ryūmachi | リューマチ |
| Ulcer | Kaiyō | 潰瘍（かいよう） |
| Wound | Kizu | 傷 |
| I am allergic to … | … ni taishite arerugi o okoshimasu | …に対してアレルギーを起こします |
| I am expecting a baby in … | … ni shussan no youtie desu | …に出産の予定です |
| My wife is expecting a baby in December | Kanai wa jū-ni-gatsu ni shussan no yotei desu | 家内は十二月に出産の予定です |
| She is expecting a baby next month | Kanojo wa raigetsu shussan no yotei desu | 彼女は来月出産の予定です |

体

# PARTS OF THE BODY

| English | Romaji | Japanese |
|---|---|---|
| Ankel | Kurubushi | くるぶし |
| Appendix | Chūyosui (Mōchō) | 虫様垂（盲腸） |
| Arm | Ude | 腕 |
| Artery | Dōmyaku | 動脈 |
| Back | Senaka | 背中 |
| Blood | Chi (Ketsueki) | 血（血液） |
| Bone/Bones | Hone | 骨 |

24

| Bowels | Chō | 腸 |
| Breast | Chibusa | 乳房 |
| Cheek | Hoo | 頬 |
| Chest | Mune | 胸 |
| Chin | Ago | あご |
| Collar-bone | Sakotsu | 鎖骨（さこつ） |
| Ear | Mimi | 耳 |
| Elbow | Hiji | ひじ |
| Eye | Me | 目 |
| Face | Kao | 顔 |
| Finger | Yubi | 指 |
| Foot | Ashi | 足 |
| Forehead | Hitai | ひたい |
| Gland | Sen | 腺 |
| A lymphatic gland | Rinpa-sen | リンパ腺 |
| The (lymphatic) glands are enlarged | Rinpa-sen ga harete iru | リンパ腺がはれている |
| Hair | Ke, Kami-no-ke | 毛、髪の毛 |
| Hand | Te | 手 |
| Heart | Shinzō | 心臓 |
| Heel | Kakato | かかと |
| Hip | Shiri | 尻 |

|  |  |  |
|---|---|---|
| Intestine | Chō | 腸 |
| Small intestine | Shōchō | 小腸 |
| Large intestine | Daichō | 大腸 |
| Jaw | Ago | あご |
| Joint | Kansetsu | 関節 |
| Kidney | Jinzō | 腎臓 |
| Knee | Hiza | ひざ |
| Knee cap | Shitsugaikotsu | 膝蓋骨 |
| Leg | Ashi | 脚 |
| Lip | Kuchibiru | 唇（くちびる） |
| Liver | Kanzō | 肝臓 |
| Lung | Hai | 肺 |
| Mouth | Kuchi | 口 |
| Muscle | Kinniku | 筋肉 |
| Neck | Kubi | 首 |
| Nerve | Shinkei | 神経 |
| Nose | Hana | 鼻 |
| Rib | Rokkotsu | 肋骨 |
| Shoulder | Kata | 肩 |
| Skin | Hifu | 皮膚 |
| Spine | Sekizui | 脊髄 |
| Stomach | I | 胃 |

|  |  |  |
|---|---|---|
| Tendon | Ken | 腱 |
| Tendon of Achilles | Akiresu-ken | アキレス腱 |
| Thigh | Momo | 腿（もも） |
| Throat | Nodo | 咽喉（のど） |
| Thumb | Oyayubi | 親指 |
| Toe | Ashi-yubi | 足指 |
| Tongue | Shita | 舌 |
| Tonsils | Hentōsen | 扁桃腺（へんとうせん） |
| Urine | Nyō | 尿 |
| Vein | Jōmyaku | 静脈 |
| Wrist | Tekubi | 手頸 |

## BOOK SHOP　本

|  |  |  |
|---|---|---|
| Do you have a guide book in Englsih? | Eigo no gaido-bukku arimau ka? | 英語のガイドブックありますか？ |
| Do you have a guide book in French? | Furansu-go ni gaido-bukku arimasu ka? | フランス語のガイドブックありますか？ |
| Of all Japan? | Nihon zenkoku no desu ka? | 日本全国のですか？ |
| Of Kyōto and Nara? | Kyōto to Nara no desu ka? | 京都と奈良のです |

| | | |
|---|---|---|
| Do you have a map of the city? | Kono machi no chizu wa arimasu ka? | この町の地図はありますか？ |
| Do you have a map of the country? | Nihon no chizu wa arimasu ka? | 日本の地図はありますか？ |

## STATIONARY SHOP

文房具

| | | |
|---|---|---|
| I would like to buy ... | ... o kaitai no desu ga | ...を買いたいのですが |
| I would like to buy a pencil | Enpitsu o kaitai no desu ga | 鉛筆を買いたいのですが |
| Fountain pen | Mannenhitsu | 万年筆 |
| Ball point pen | Bōru-pen | ボールペン |
| Refill for the pen | Pen no kae-shin | ペンの替芯（かえしん） |
| Envelopes | Fūtō | 封筒 |
| Eraser | Keshi-gomu | 消しゴム |
| Writing pad | Binsen | 便箋 |
| String, Cord | Himo | ひも |
| Paper | Kami | 紙 |

# COLORS 色

|  |  |  |
|---|---|---|
| Black | Kuro | 黒 |
| Blue | Ao | 青 |
| Brown | Chairo | 茶色 |
| Gray | Haiiro, Gurei | 灰色, グレイ |
| Green | Midori | 緑 |
| Pink | Pinku | ピンク |
| Purple | Murasaki | 紫 |
| Red | Aka | 赤 |
| White | Shiro | 白 |
| Yellow | Kiiro | 黄色 |

# HAIRDRESSER 散髪

|  |  |  |
|---|---|---|
| I want to get a hair cut | Kami o kitte kudasai | 髪を切って下さい |
| How do you want it cut? | Dono yōni kirimashō ka? | どのように切りましょうか? |
| I want to get a hair cut ... | ...(no kami) o kitte kudasai | ...(の髪)を切って下さい |
| In front | Mae no kami o | 前の髪を |

| On the sides | Wakino kami o | わきの髪を |
|---|---|---|
| Behind | Ushiro no kami o | 後の髪を |
| Short | Mijikaku | 短く |
| Not too short | Amari mijikasuginai yōni | あまり短かすぎないように |
| Longer | Nagaku | 長く |
| Beard | Ago-hige | あごひげ |
| Moustache | Kuchi-hige | 口ひげ |
| I want a shampoo, please | Senpatsu o onegai shimasu | 洗髪をお願いします |
| Don't cut it too short ... | ... wa amari mijikaku kirisuginai yōni shite-kudasai | …はあまり短かく切りすぎないようにして下さい |
| Don't cut it too short in front | Mae wa amari mijikaku kirisuginai yōni shite-kudasai | 前はあまり短かく切りすぎないようにして下さい |
| At the back | Ushiro wa | 後は |
| At the sides | Waki wa | わきは |
| On top | Ue wa | 上は |
| Don't use the clippers | Barikan wa tsukawanai de kudasai | バリカンは使わないで下さい |
| Just a trim, please | Soroeru dake ni shite kudasai | そろえるだけにして下さい |
| Would you please trim ... | ... o soroete kudasai | …をそろえて下さい |
| That's enough off | Sore de jūbun desu | それで十分です |
| Do you want any cream? | Kurīmu o o-tsuke shimashō ka? | クリームをおつけしましょうか? |

Do you want any lotion? | Rōshon o o-tsuke shimashō ka? | ローションをおつけしましょうか？

Yes, please | Hai onegai shimasu | はい、おねがいします
Thank you | Arigatō | ありがとう
How much do I owe you? | Ikura desu ka? | いくらですか？

# RESTAURANT

レストラン

Can you recommend a good restaurant? | Dokoka ii resutoran o gozonji desu ka? | どこかいいレストランをご存知ですか？
Restaurant | Resutoran | レストラン
A good restaurant | Ii resutoran | いいレストラン
A good Japanese restaurant | Ii nihon-ryōri-ten | いい日本料理店
A good Chinese restaurant | Ii chūka-ryōri-ten | いい中華料理店
Do you know any unexpensive Japanese restaurant? | Amari takaku-nai nihon-ryōri-ten o gozonji desu ka? | あまり高くない日本料理店をご存知ですか？
Could we have a table by the window? | Madogiwa ni seki o toremasu ka? | 窓ぎわに席をとれますか？
By the window | Madogiwa ni | 窓ぎわに
How many persons? | Nanmei-sama desu ka? | 何名さまですか？

|  |  |  |
|---|---|---|
| Two persons | Futari desu | 二人です |
| Three persons | San-nin desu | 三人です |
| Four persons | Yo-nin desu | 四人です |
| Five persons | Go-nin desu | 五人です |
| Six persons | Roku-nin desu | 六人です |
| Could I/we have an ashtray? | Haizara o motte-kite-itadakemasu ka? | 灰皿をもってきていただけますか？ |
| Ashtray | Haizara | 灰皿 |
| Another chair | Isu o mō hitotsu | 椅子をもう一つ |
| Fork | Fōku | フォーク |
| Glass | Koppu | コップ |
| Glass of water | Mizu o koppu ni ippai | 水をコップに一杯 |
| Knife | Naifu | ナイフ |
| Napkin | Napukin | ナプキン |
| Spoon | Supūn | スプーン |
| Toothpick | Tsumayōji | つまようじ |
| Would you bring us some bread, please? | Pan o sukoshi itadakemasu ka? | パンを少しいただけますか？ |
| Bread | Pan | パン |
| Butter | Batā | バター |
| Jam | Jamu | ジャム |
| Mustard | Karashi | からし |

32

| | | |
|---|---|---|
| Olive-oil | Orību-oiru | オリーブオイル |
| Pepper | Koshō | こしょう |
| Rolls | Maki-pan | 巻きパン |
| Salt | Shio | 塩 |
| Sugar | Satō | さとう |
| Water | Mizu | 水 |
| I'd like to have ... | ... o itadakitai | ... をいただきたい |
| Have you any ... | ... wa arimasu ka? | ... はありますか？ |
| What kind of ... do you have? | Dono yōna ... ga arimasu ka? | どのような・・・がありますか？ |

## SOUP

スープ

| | | |
|---|---|---|
| Chicken soup | Tori-sūpu | 鶏スープ |
| Clear soup | Konsome | コンソメ |
| Mushroom soup | Masshurūmu (Kinoko)-sūpu | マッシュルーム（きのこ）スープ |
| Tomato soup | Tomato-sūpu | トマトスープ |
| Vegetable soup | Yasai-supu | 野菜スープ |

# EGGS

たまご料理

| | | |
|---|---|---|
| Boiled eggs | Yude-tamago | ゆで卵 |
| Medium | Hanjuku | 半熟（はんじゅく） |
| Hard | Katayude | かたゆで |
| Fried eggs | Medama-yaki | 目玉焼き |
| Scrambled | Iritamago (Sukuranburu) | いり玉子（スクランブル） |
| Omlet, plain | Omuretsu | オムレツ |
| Ham omlet | Hamu-omuretsu | ハムオムレツ |

# FISH AND SHELLS

魚貝類

| | | |
|---|---|---|
| Crab | Kani | 蟹（かに） |
| Lobster | Ise-ebi | 伊勢海老 |
| Oyster | Kaki | 牡蠣（かき） |
| Roast fish | Yaki-zakana | 焼き魚 |
| Salmon | Sake | 鮭（さけ） |
| Sardine | Iwashi | いわし |
| Shrimp | Ko-ebi | 小海老 |
| Sole | Shitabirame | 舌平目 |

34

# MEAT

肉 料 理

|  |  |  |
|---|---|---|
| Bacon | Bēkon | ベーコン |
| Beef | Bifu | ビーフ（牛肉） |
| Beef cutlet | Bifu katsuretsu | ビーフカツレツ |
| Beef stew | Bifu shichū | ビーフシチュー |
| Beefsteak | Bifuteki | ビフテキ |
| Rare | Nama-yaki | なま焼き |
| Medium | Chū-yaki, Midiam | 中焼き |
| Well-done | Hon-yaki | 本焼き |
| Chicken | Toriniku | 鶏肉 |
| Grilled chicken | Toriniku guriru | 鶏肉グリル |
| Young chicken | Wakadori | 若鶏 |
| Croquette | Korokke | コロッケ |
| Cutlets | Katsuretsu | カツレツ |
| Ham | Hamu | ハム |
| Lamb | Kohitsuji | 小羊 |
| Pork | Pōku | ポーク（豚肉） |
| Pork chops | Pōku choppu | ポークチョップ |
| Roast pork | Yaki-buta | 焼豚 |

| | | |
|---|---|---|
| Sausage | Sōsēji | ソーセージ |
| Stew | Shichū | シチュー |
| Veal | Koushi | 犢肉（子牛） |

## VEGETABLE 野菜

| | | |
|---|---|---|
| Asparagas | Asuparagasu | アスパラガス |
| Cabbage | Kyabetsu | キャベツ |
| Cauliflower | Karifurawā | カリフラワー |
| Carrot | Ninjin | にんじん |
| Cucumber | Kyuri | きゅうり |
| Garlic | Ninniku | にんにく |
| Without garlic | Ninniku-nuki | にんにく抜き |
| Green peas | Gurînpîsu | グリンピース |
| Lettus | Retasu | レタス |
| Mushroom | Kinoko | きのこ |
| Onions | Tamanegi | 玉ねぎ |
| Raw, sliced onions | Tamanegi no nama-kizami | 玉ねぎの生きざみ |
| Potatoes | Poteto | ポテト |
| Boiled potatoes | Boirudo-poteto | ボイルドポテト |

36

| Fried potatoes | Poteto-furai | ポテトフライ |
| Mashed potatoes | Masshu-poteto | マッシュポテト |
| Salad | Sarada | サラダ |
| Spinach | Hōrensō | ほうれん草 |
| Tomato | Tomato | トマト |

## FRUIT AND DESERT

果物とデザート

| Apple | Ringo | リンゴ |
| Banana | Banana | バナナ |
| Cheese | Chīzu | チーズ |
| Fresh fruit | Fureshu-furūtsu | フレッシュフルーツ |
| Fruit salad | Furūtsu-sarada | フルーツサラダ |
| Grapefruit | Gurēpu-furūtsu | グレープフルーツ |
| Ice cream | Aisukurīmu | アイスクリーム |
| Vanila | Banira | バニラ |
| Chocolate | Chokorēto | チョコレート |
| Lemon | Remon | レモン |
| Orange | Orenji | オレンジ |
| Pineapple | Painappuru | パイナップル |

Stewed fruit　　　　　　　　Furūtsu-shichū　　　　フルーツシチュー
Strawberries　　　　　　　　Ichigo　　　　　　　　　イチゴ

## BEVERAGES

飲　　物

| | | |
|---|---|---|
| Beer | Bīru | ビール |
| Brandy | Burandē | ブランデー |
| Cognac | Konyakku | コニャック |
| Cocoa | Kokoa | ココア |
| Coffee | Kōhī | コーヒー |
| Green tea (Japanese tea) | Ryokucha | 緑茶 |
| Juice | Jūsu | ジュース |
| Orange juice | Orenji-jūsu | オレンジジュース |
| Tomato juice | Tomato-jūsu | トマトジュース |
| Milk | Miruku | ミルク |
| With milk | Miruku-iri | ミルク入り |
| Hot milk | Atsui miruku | 熱いミルク |
| Cold milk | Tsumetai miruku | 冷たいミルク |
| Tea | Cha | 茶 |
| Water | Mizu | 水 |
| Whisky | Uiski | ウイスキー |
| Wine | Wain | ワイン |

38

# MISCELLANEOUS

其 の 他

|  |  |  |
|---|---|---|
| Baked | Yakimono | 焼物 |
| Boiled | Nimono, Yudemono | 煮物, ゆでもの |
| Cold, chilled | Tsumetai | 冷たい |
| Fresh | Shinsen-na | 新鮮な |
| Fried | Furai | フライ |
| Grilled | Yaki-mono, guriru | 焼き物, グリル |
| Hashed | Hayashi | はやし |
| Hot | Atsui | 熱い |
| Ice | Kōri, Aisu | 氷, アイス |
| Mashed | Masshu | マッシュ |
| Rice | Raisu | ライス |
| Roast | Rōsuto | ロースト |
| Steamed | Mushimono | むし物 |

# JAPANESE FOOD

日本料理

|  |  |  |
|---|---|---|
| Sliced (slices of) raw fish | Sashimi | さしみ |
| Fatty (oily) tuna meat | Toro | とろ |
| Sliced tuna | Maguro no sashimi | まぐろのさしみ |
| Tuna | Maguro | まぐろ |
| Roast chicken | Yakitori | やきとり |
| "Sukiyaki" | Sukiyaki | すきやき |
| "Sushi" (vinegared fish and rice) | Sushi | 鮨（すし） |
| Hand-rolled "Sushi" | Nigirizushi | 握り鮨（にぎりずし） |
| Horse-radish | Wasabi | わさび |
| "Tōfu" (soy bean curd) | Tōfu | 豆腐（とうふ） |
| Soy | Shōyu | 醤油（しょうゆ） |
| (A pair of) chopsticks | Hashi | 箸（はし） |

## TIME, DAYS, MONTHS

時間、日、月

|  |  |  |
|---|---|---|
| Morning | Asa | 朝 |
| In the morning | Gozen | 午前 |
| Noon | Shōgo (or Hiru) | 正午、昼 |
| At noon | Shōgo ni | 正午に |
| Afternoon | Gogo | 午後 |
| Daytime | Hiru | 昼 |
| In the afternoon | Gogo ni | 午後に |
| Evening | Yūgata | 夕方 |
| In the evening | Yūgata ni | 夕方に |
| Night | Yoru | 夜 |
| Mid-night | Mayonaka | 真夜中 |
| Last night | Sakuya | 昨夜（さくや） |
| The day before yesterday | Ototoi (or Issakujitsu) | おととい（一昨日） |
| Yesterday | Kinō (or Sakujitsu) | 昨日 |
| Today | Kyō (or Honjitsu) | 今日 |
| Tomorrow | Asu, Ashita | 明日（あす）, あした |
| Tomorrow morning | Myōchō | 明朝 |
| Tomorrow afternoon | Asu no gogo | あすの午後 |
| The day after tomorrow | Asatte | あさって |

|  |  |  |
|---|---|---|
| Now | Ima | 今 |
| What time is it now? | Ima nan-ji deshō ka? | 今何時でしょうか？ |
| It's one o'clock | Ichi-ji desu | 一時です |
| One o'clock | Ichi-ji | 一時 |
| Two o'clock | Ni-ji | 二時 |
| Three o'clock | San-ji | 三時 |
| Four o'clock | Yo-ji | 四時 |
| Five o'clock | Go-ji | 五時 |
| Six o'clock | Roku-ji | 六時 |
| Seven o'clock | Shichi-ji | 七時 |
| Eight o'clock | Hachi-ji | 八時 |
| Nine o'clock | Ku-ji | 九時 |
| Ten o'clock | Jū-ji | 十時 |
| Eleven o'clock | Jūichi-ji | 十一時 |
| Twelve o'clock | Jūni-ji | 十二時 |
| Ten past three | San-ji ju-ppun sugi | 三時十分過ぎ |
| A quarter past five | Goji jūgo-fun sugi | 五時十五分過ぎ |
| Half past six | Roku-ji-han | 六時半 |
| Seven twenty | Shichi-ji niju-ppun | 七時二十分 |
| Twenty past seven | Shichi-ji niju-pun sugi | 七時二十分過ぎ |
| Seven forty | Shichi-ji yonju-ppun | 七時四十分 |
| Twenty to eight | Hachi-ji niju-ppun mae | 八時二十分前 |

42

|  |  |  |
|---|---|---|
| Nine forty-five | Ku-ji yonjū-go-fun | 九時四十五分 |
| A quarter to ten | Jū-ji jū-go-fun mae | 十時十五分前 |
| At what time does the museum open? | Hakubutsukan wa nanji ni akimasu ka? | 博物館は何時に開きますか? |
| Museum | Hakubutsukan | 博物館 |
| Office | Ofisu, Jimusho | オフィス、事務所 |
| Theater | Gekijō | 劇場 |
| Department store | Depāto | デパート |
| The/This shop | Kono mise | この店 |
| When will this shop be closed? | Kono mise wa itsu shimarimasu ka? | この店はいつ閉まりますか? |
| The department store is closed today | Depāto wa kyō wa shimatte imasu | デパートは今日は閉まっています |
| Because today is holiday | Kyō wa yasumi dakara desu | 今日は休日だからです |
| Holiday | Kyūjitsu (or Yasumi) | 休日、休み |
| What day of the week is it today? | Kyō wa nanyōbi desu ka? | 今日は何曜日ですか? |
| Today is Sunday | Kōy wa nichi-yōbi desu | 今日は日曜日です |
| Sunday | Nichi-yōbi | 日曜日 |
| Monday | Getsu-yōbi | 月曜日 |
| Tuesday | Kayō-bi | 火曜日 |
| Wednesday | Sui-yōbi | 水曜日 |

| | | |
|---|---|---|
| Thursday | Moku-yō-bi | 木曜日 |
| Friday | Kin-yōbi | 金曜日 |
| Saturday | Do-yōbi | 土曜日 |
| A week | Isshū | 一週 |
| For a week | Isshūkan | 一週間 |
| Last week | Sen-shū | 先週 |
| This week | Kon-shū | 今週 |
| Next week | Rai-shū | 来週 |
| When the exhibition will be opened? | Tenjikai wa itsu hirakaremasu ka? | 展示会はいつ開かれますか？ |
| On Tuesday of this week | Konshū no kayō-bi desu | 今週の火曜日です |
| From next Friday | Raishū no kinyōbi kara desu | 来週の金曜日からです |
| How long? | Donokurai no kikan desu ka? | どの位の期間ですか？ |
| For three weeks | Sanshū-kan desu | 三週間（です） |
| About | Yaku (or Ooyoso) | 約、およそ |
| For a month | Hitotsuki-kan desu | ひと月間（です） |
| Month | Tsuki | 月 |
| Last month | Sen-getsu | 先月 |
| This month | Kon-getsu | 今月 |
| Next month | Rai-getsu | 来月 |
| January | Ichi-gatsu | 一月 |
| February | Ni-gatsu | 二月 |

44

|  |  |  |
|---|---|---|
| March | San-gatsu | 三月 |
| April | Shi-gatsu | 四月 |
| May | Go-gatsu | 五月 |
| June | Roku-gatsu | 六月 |
| July | Shichi-gatsu | 七月 |
| August | Hachi-gatsu | 八月 |
| September | Ku-gatsu | 九月 |
| October | Jū-gatsu | 十月 |
| November | Jūichi-gatsu | 十一月 |
| December | Jūni-gatsu | 十二月 |
| Season | Kisetsu | 季節 |
| Four seasons | Shiki | 四季 |
| Spring | Haru | 春 |
| Summer | Natsu | 夏 |
| Autumn | Aki | 秋 |
| Winter | Fuyu | 冬 |
| In spring | Haru ni | 春に |
| Year | Toshi | 年 |
| Last year | Sakunen | 昨年 |
| This year | Kotoshi | 今年 |
| Next Year | Rainen | 来年 |

| English | Rōmaji | Japanese |
|---|---|---|
| | | 天候 |
| It's a beautiful day today, isn't it? | Kyō wa subarashii hi desu ne | 今日はすばらしい日ですね |
| What a beautiful day! | Nanto subarashii hi deshō! | なんとすばらしい日でしょう！ |
| Beautiful | Subarashii, Utsukushii | すばらしい、美しい |
| Beautiful sunset | Utsukushii yūyake | 美しい夕焼け |
| The sun is shining | Hi ga yoku tette imasu | 日がよく照っています |
| Bright | Hareta | 晴れた |
| Bright and clear | Yoku hareta | よく晴れた |
| A bright and clear day | Yoku hareta hi | よく晴れた日 |
| Chilly | Hiebie shita | 冷え冷えした |
| Cloudy | Kumotta | 曇った |
| Cold | Samui | 寒い |
| Very cold | Taihen samui | 大変寒い |
| Today is very cold | Kyō wa hontō-ni samui desu | 今日は本当に寒いです |
| Dry | Kawaita | 乾いた |
| Foggy | Kiri ga fukai | 霧が深い |
| Hot | Atsui | 暑い |
| Very hot | Taihen atsui | 大変暑い |
| Humidity | Shikki | 湿気 |

46

| Sultry | Mushi-atsui | 蒸暑い（むしあつい） |
| Rain | Ame | 雨 |
| It is raining | Ame ga futte-imasu | 雨が降っています |
| Snow | Yuki | 雪 |
| It is snowing | Yuki ga futte-imasu | 雪が降っています |
| Typhoon | Taifū | 台風 |
| Typhoon is approaching | Taifu ga chikazuite-imasu | 台風が近づいています |
| Warm | Atatakai | 暖かい |
| Wind | Kaze | 風 |
| Umbrella | Kasa | かさ |
| Raincoat | Reinkōto | レインコート |
| Rubber boots | Gomugutsu | ゴムぐつ |
| Rain shoes | Amagutsu | 雨ぐつ |
| Should I take an umbrella with me? | Kasa o motte-ikubeki deshō ka? | かさを持っていくべきでしょうか？ |

| CLOTHES | | |
|---|---|---|

| I would like to buy ... | ... o kaitai no desu ga | ... を買いたいのですが |
| My size is ... | Watashi no saizu wa ... desu | 私のサイズは... です |
| May I try it on? | Kite-mite-mo ii desu ka? | 着てみてもいいですか? |
| It is too long | Naga-sugimasu | 長すぎます |
| It is too short | Mijika-sugimasu | 短かすぎます |
| It is too narrow | Sema-sugimasu | せますぎます |
| It is too wide | Hiro-sugimasu | 広すぎます |
| A pair of shorts | Tanzubon | 短ズボン |
| A pair of trousers | Zubon | ズボン |
| Button | Botan | ボタン |
| Cape | Kēpu | ケープ |
| Coat | Kōto | コート |
| Gloves | Tebukuro | 手袋 |
| Handkerchief | Hankechi | ハンケチ |
| Jacket | Jaketsu | ジャケツ |
| Leather | Nameshigawa | なめし皮 |
| Linen | Asanuno (or Rinneru) | 麻布。リンネル |
| Pocket | Poketto | ポケット |
| Pijamas | Pajama | パジャマ |

衣　服

48

| English | Rōmaji | Japanese |
|---|---|---|
| Rain coat | Renkōto | レインコート |
| Scarf | Sukāfu | スカーフ |
| Silk | Kinu | 絹 |
| Stockings | Sutokking | ストッキング |
| Suit | Sūtsu | スーツ, 背広 |
| Sweater | Sētā | セーター |
| Swimming suit | Mizugi | 水着 |
| Tie | Nekutai | ネクタイ |

# LAUNDRY

クリーニング

| English | Rōmaji | Japanese |
|---|---|---|
| Could you, please, clean my shirt? | Shatsu o aratte itadakemasu ka? | シャツを洗っていただけますか? |
| Shirt/Shirts | Shatsu | シャツ |
| Collar | Karā | カラー |
| Dress | Doresu | ドレス |
| Underwear | Shitagi | 下着 |
| Could you wash and iron the shirts for me? | Shatsu o aratte airon o kakete itadake-masu ka? | シャツを洗ってアイロンをかけていただけますか |
| Until tomorrow | Asu made-ni | 明日までに |
| When will they be ready? | Itsu made-ni dekiagari masu ka? | いつまでに出来上りますか? |

49

# CAR RENTAL

レンタカー

| English | Rōmaji | Japanese |
|---|---|---|
| Where can I rent a car? | Kuruma o kariru-niwa dōshitara ii deshō ka? | 車を借りるにはどうしたらいいでしょうか？ |
| I have an international driving license | Kokusai-menkyoshō o motte-imasu | 国際免許証を持っています |
| How much is it to rent a car per day? | Kuruma o ichinichi karitara dono-kurai shimasu ka? | 車を一日借りたらどの位しますか？ |
| Where is the nearest petrol (gas) station? | Koko kara ichiban chikai gasorin-sutando wa doko desu ka? | ここから　一番近いガソリンスタンドはどこですか？ |
| Please, put in ... liters | ... rittoru irete kudasai | …　リットル入れて下さい |
| Check the oil, please | Oiru o shirabete kudasai | オイルを調べて下さい |
| Oil | Oiru (or Abura) | オイル、油 |
| Brakes | Burēki | ブレーキ |
| Gear box | Hensokuki (or Giya) | 変速機（ギヤ） |
| Plugs | Puragu | プラグ |
| Please put the water in ... | ... ni mizu o irete kudasai | …　に水を入れて下さい |
| Battery | Batterī | バッテリー |
| Radiator | Rajietā | ラジエター |
| Change the lubricating oil in the car | Junkatsu-yu o irete kudasai | 潤滑油を入れ換えて下さい |

50

51

| Clutch | Kuracchi | クラッチ |
| Road | Dōro (*or* Michi) | 道路、道 |
| Bad road | Akuro | 悪路 |
| Narrow road | Semai dōro | 狭い道路 |
| Crossroad | Kōsaten | 交差点 |
| Bridge | Hashi | 橋 |
| Turn | Tān | ターン |
| Sharp curve | Kyū kābu | 急カーブ |

## NUMBERS

数字

| 1 | Ichi | 一 |
| 2 | Ni | 二 |
| 3 | San | 三 |
| 4 | Shi | 四 |
| 5 | Go | 五 |
| 6 | Roku | 六 |
| 7 | Shichi | 七 |
| 8 | Hachi | 八 |
| 9 | Ku | 九 |
| 10 | Jū | 十 |

| | | |
|---|---|---|
| 11 | 十一 | Jū-ichi |
| 12 | 十二 | Jū-ni |
| 13 | 十三 | Jū-san |
| 14 | 十四 | Jū-shi |
| 15 | 十五 | Jū-go |
| 16 | 十六 | Jū-roku |
| 17 | 十七 | Jū-shichi |
| 18 | 十八 | Jū-hachi |
| 19 | 十九 | Jū-ku |
| 20 | 二十 | Nijū |
| 30 | 三十 | Sanjū |
| 40 | 四十 | Yonjū |
| 50 | 五十 | Gojū |
| 60 | 六十 | Rokujū |
| 70 | 七十 | Shichijū |
| 80 | 八十 | Hachijū |
| 90 | 九十 | Kyūjū |
| 100 | 百 | Hyaku |
| 101 | 百一 | Hyaku-ichi |
| 200 | 二百 | Nihyaku |
| 1,000 | 千 | Sen |
| 10,000 | 一万 | Ichi-man |
| 100,000 | 十万 | Jū-man |

52

## SOME SAYINGS

| | |
|---|---|
| Tabi wa michizure, yo wa nasake | No road is weary with company, nor life with sympathy |
| Kawaii ko niwa tabi o saseyo | Spare the rod and spoil the child |
| Hyakubun wa ikken ni shikazu | Seeing is believing |
| Masaka no tomo wa shin no tomo | A friend in need is a friend indeed |
| Koketsu ni irazunba koji o ezu | Nothing venture, nothing have |
| Tade kuu mushi mo sukizuki | There is no accounting for tastes |
| Fuku-sui bon ni kaerazu | It is no use crying over spilt milk |
| Kōbō ni mo fude no ayamari | Even Homer sometimes nods |
| Shippai wa seikō no moto | Failure is the turning point toward success |